JUMPIN' JIM
Ukule COUNTRY

COMPILED AND ARRANGED BY JIM BELOFF

G000293393

HAL•LEONARD®
CORPORATION
7777 W. BLUEMOUND RD. P.O. BOX 13819 MILWAUKEE, WI 53213

Edited by Ronny S. Schiff
Cover and Art Direction by Elizabeth Maihock Beloff
Graphics and Music Typography by Charylu Roberts

FOREWORD

Howdy! Welcome to the "Lazy U Ranch." Somewhere we have a list of chores to do, but right now we're content to strum away the day. It was only a matter of time before we discovered just how good country and western songs can sound on a ukulele. As always, some tunes shine especially bright when played on the uke and those are the ones we've collected here. Most are well known classics from the '40s, '50s and '60s and are easy to play with a minimum of chord changes.

Although the ukulele is not normally associated with country music, there are some connections if you look. Legendary Nashville guitarist, Chet Atkins, started out on a ukulele and "The Singing Brakeman" Jimmie Rodgers played uke and recorded with Lani McIntyre's Hawaiians in the early '30s. Also, Marty Robbins is pictured playing a baritone uke on the back of his "Return Of The Gunfighter" album.

We had a posse of song wranglers assisting us with this collection. Our biggest thank you goes to Dr. Deb Porter, a strummer and scholar from Texas, who helped us start and then winnow down the song list. Her immediate and continuing enthusiasm for this project (and Austin photos) played a big part in its birth. Also, many thanks to Cowboy Jack Clement, Roger Cook, Rick Cunha, Larry Dilg, George Gruhn, Sid Hausman, Doug Haverty, Mimi Kennedy, Ron Middlebrook, Lee Ann Photoglo and Peter Wingerd. Special thanks to those three cowgirl sweethearts Liz Beloff, Charylu Roberts and Ronny Schiff.

—Jumpin' Jim Beloff
Los Angeles, CA 2005

For all inquiries: Flea Market Music, Inc., Box 1127, Studio City, CA. 91614.
Visit us on the web at www.fleamarketmusic.com

On the road to
★ NASHVILLE ★

LOOKING FOR UKES IN ALL THE WRONG PLACES

Few go to Nashville, Tennessee looking for ukuleles. In the land of guitars, banjos, fiddles and mandolins, it's a little like looking for a needle in a haystack. Nonetheless, while working on this songbook, we headed off to Music City with high hopes. Lo and behold, we found a few. Our report...

British songwriter, **Roger Cook** picked up a baritone ukulele in the early '60s and hasn't stopped strumming. With partner Roger Greenaway, the two penned a lot of hit songs during the British Invasion including "You've Got Your Troubles" for the Fortunes and "Long Cool Woman (In A Black Dress)" for the Hollies. In the '70s, Cook moved to Nashville where he co-wrote the hits "Talking In Your Sleep" for Crystal Gayle and "I Believe In You" for Don Williams. Many of his biggest hits have been written on uke including the New Seeker's "I'd Like To Teach The World To Sing," which started out as a Coca-Cola jingle. Cook thinks of his ukulele as "a little friend you can carry under your arm" and admits that after 43 years of playing he has yet to get a callus.

Born in Memphis, Tennessee in 1931, **Cowboy Jack Clement** is a country music Renaissance man with major credits as a songwriter, producer, recording studio pioneer, music publisher and artist. In 1956, Clement found work at Sun Records as an engineer on recording sessions with Roy Orbison, Johnny Cash, and Jerry Lee Lewis. He also wrote two of Cash's hits, "Ballad Of A Teenage Queen" and "Guess Things Happen That Way." Over the years, he worked for Chet Atkins and discovered and recorded Charley Pride and Don Williams. At times, he has also added ukulele to certain tracks he's produced, claiming that it gives a certain "ping" to the overall sound. Clement is a colorful character and even has a custom uke that looks like a miniature Gibson J200 guitar.

Elvis sighting in Nashville! If **Elvis Presley** were alive today, we'd like to think he would have found this Flame Fluke just perfect for some hot licks.

According to many, **George Gruhn** knows more about vintage guitars than anyone on the planet. In 1970, he established Gruhn Guitars in Nashville as one of the largest dealers of vintage instruments in the world. As such, Gruhn often has fine vintage ukuleles in its inventory as well (here he holds an extremely nice Martin 5K).

3

CHORD CORRAL

Tune Ukulele
G C E A

MAJOR CHORDS

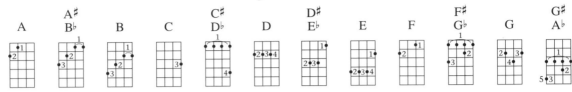

MINOR CHORDS

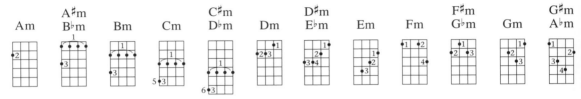

DOMINANT SEVENTH CHORDS

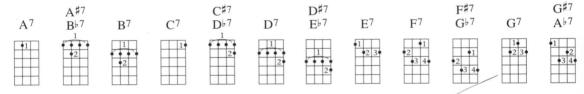

MINOR SEVENTH CHORDS

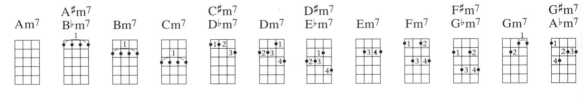

DIMINISHED SEVENTH CHORDS (dim)

AUGMENTED FIFTH CHORDS (aug or +)

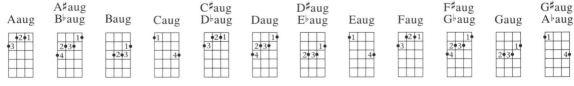

Act Naturally

Words and Music by
JOHNNY RUSSELL and VONIE MORRISON

FIRST NOTE

1. They're gon - na put me in the
2. make a score a - bout a man that's sad and

mov - ies, they're gon - na make a
lone - ly, and beg - gin' down up -

big star out of me. We'll
on his bend - ed knee. I'll

make a scene a - bout a man that's sad and lone - ly,
play the part but I won't need re - hears - in',

and all I got - ta do is act nat - 'ral -
'cause all I have to do is act nat - 'ral -

5

Well, I hope you come___ and see me in___ the

mov - ies,_____ then I know___ that

you will plain-ly see_____ the big-gest fool___ that

ev - er hit___ the big time_____ and

all I got-ta do is act nat - 'ral ly._____

"COUNTRY MUSIC IS THREE CHORDS AND THE TRUTH."

— *Harlan Howard, songwriter*

Any Time

Words and Music by
HERBERT HAPPY LAWSON

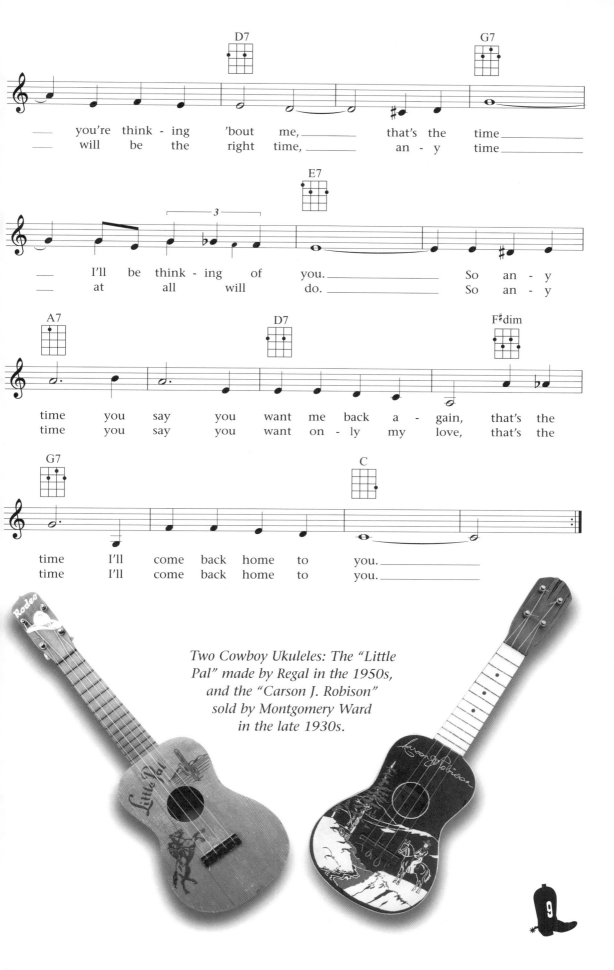

D7 G7

you're think - ing 'bout me, _____ that's the time _____
will be the right time, _____ an - y time _____

E7

I'll be think - ing of you. _____ So an - y
at all will do. _____ So an - y

A7 D7 F#dim

time you say you want me back a - gain, that's the
time you say you want on - ly my love, that's the

G7 C

time I'll come back home to you. _____
time I'll come back home to you. _____

Two Cowboy Ukuleles: The "Little Pal" made by Regal in the 1950s, and the "Carson J. Robison" sold by Montgomery Ward in the late 1930s.

Are You Lonesome Tonight?

Words and Music by
ROY TURK and LOU HANDMAN

bare?   Do you   gaze   at   your   door - step   and   pic - ture   me

there?   Is your   heart   filled   with   pain,   shall   I   come   back   a -

gain?   Tell   me,   dear,   are   you   lone - some   to - night?_____

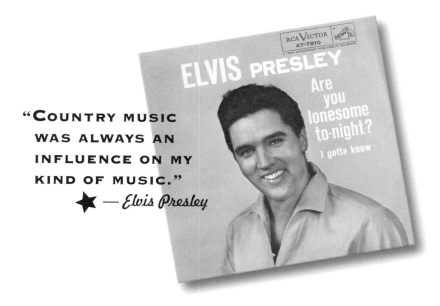

"COUNTRY MUSIC WAS ALWAYS AN INFLUENCE ON MY KIND OF MUSIC."

★ *— Elvis Presley*

ELVIS COUNTRY

Back In The Saddle Again

Words and Music by
GENE AUTRY and RAY WHITLEY

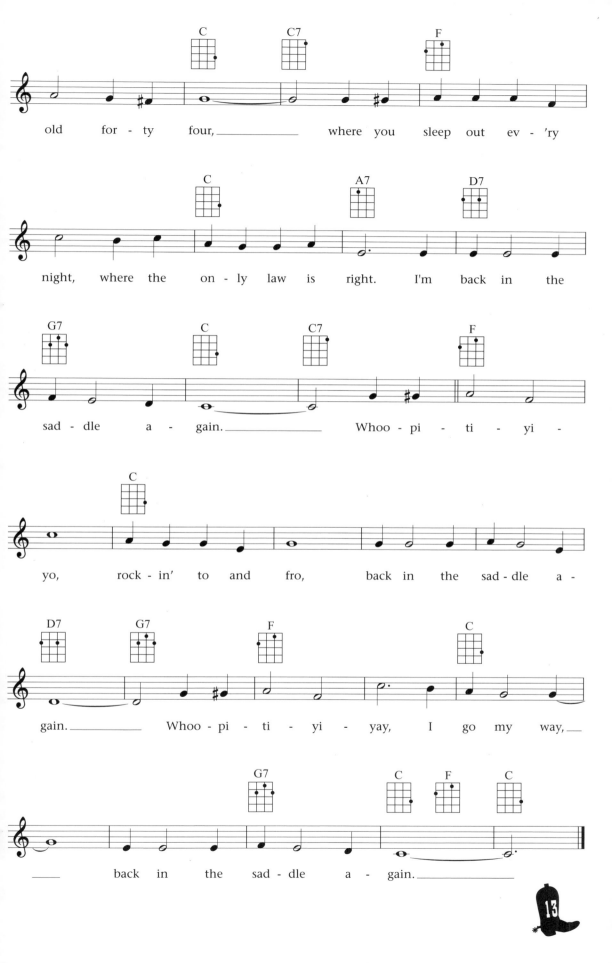

Bye Bye Love

Words and Music by FELICE BRYANT
and BOUDLEAUX BRYANT

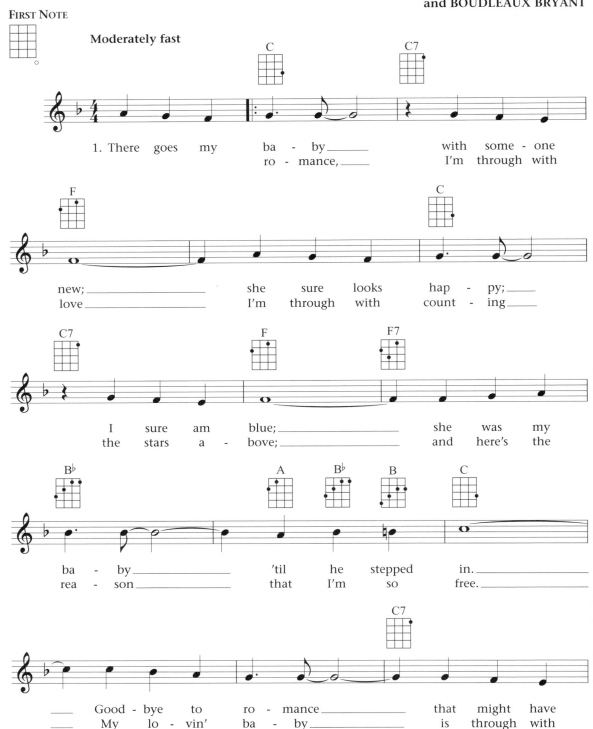

1. There goes my ba - by_____ with some - one
   ro - mance,_____ I'm through with

new;_____ she sure looks hap - py;_____
love_____ I'm through with count - ing_____

I sure am blue;_____ she was my
the stars a - bove;_____ and here's the

ba - by_____ 'til he stepped in._____
rea - son_____ that I'm so free._____

_____ Good - bye to ro - mance_____ that might have
_____ My lo - vin' ba - by_____ is through with

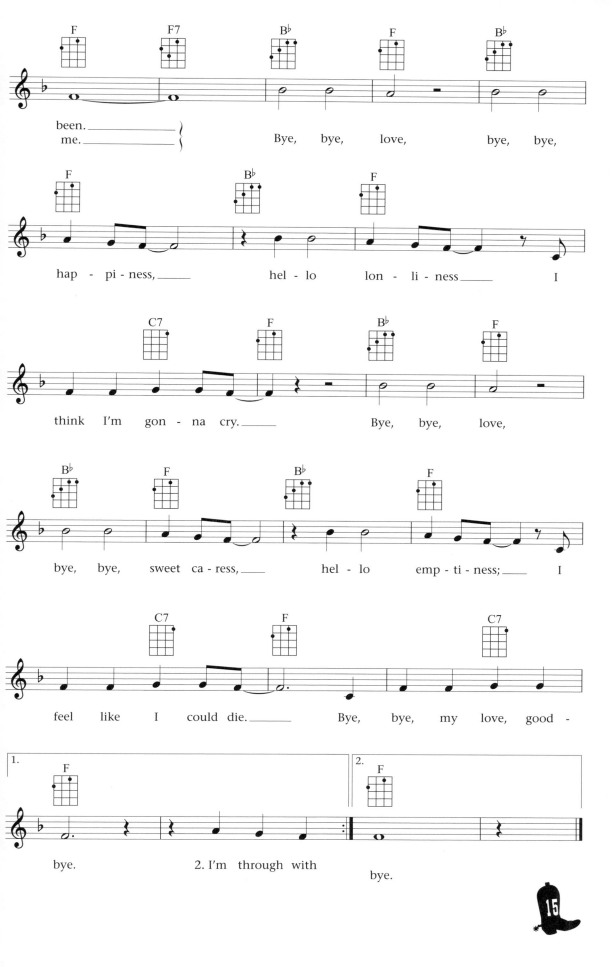

Cold, Cold Heart

Words and Music by
HANK WILLIAMS

FIRST NOTE

Moderately

1. I tried so hard, my dear, to show that
nev - er know how much it hurts to

you're my ev - 'ry dream. Yet you're a - fraid each
see you sit and cry. You know you need and

thing I do is just some e - vil scheme. A
want my love, yet you're a - fraid to try. Why

mem - 'ry from your lone - some past keeps us so far a -
do you run and hide from life? To try it just ain't

part. Why can't I free your doubt - ful mind and
smart. Why can't I free your doubt - ful mind and

16

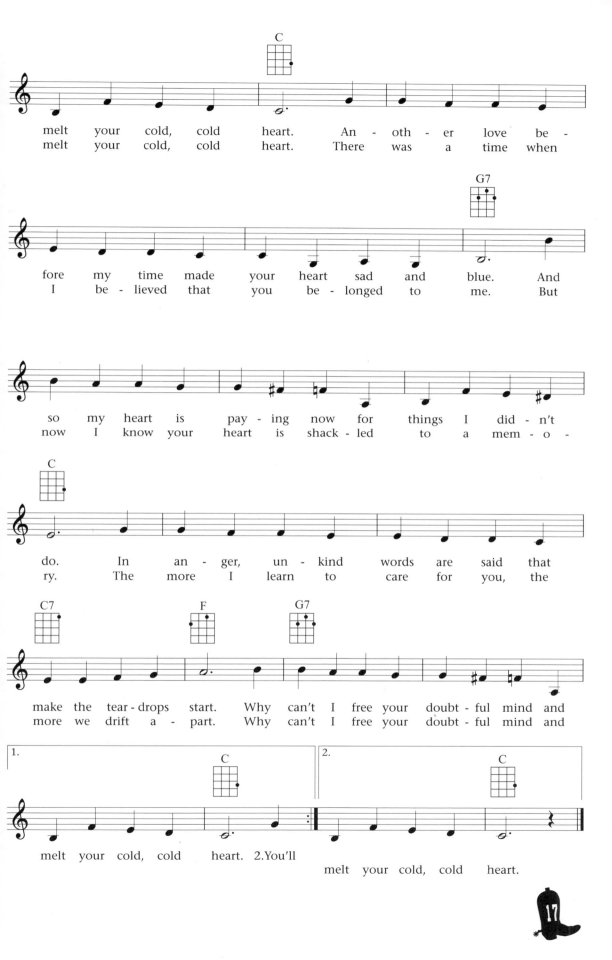

Crazy

Words and Music by
WILLIE NELSON

Moderately slow

Cra - zy, _____ cra - zy for feel - in' so lone - ly, _____

_____ I'm cra - zy, _____ cra - zy for feel - in' so

blue. _____ I knew _____ you'd love me as long as you

want - ed, _____ and then some - day _____ you'd

leave me for some - bod - y new. _____ Wor - ry, _____

why do I let my-self wor-ry, _____

won-d'rin' _____ what in the world did I do? _____

_____ Cra-zy, _____ for think-ing that my love could

hold you, _____ I'm cra-zy for try-in',

cra-zy for cry-in', and I'm cra-zy for lov-in' you!

Crying

Words and Music by
ROY ORBISON and JOE MELSON

Crying Time

Words and Music by
BUCK OWENS

1. Oh it's cry-ing time a-gain _____ you're gon-na
say that ab-sence makes _____ the heart grow

leave me, I can see that far a-way look in your eyes. I can
fond-er, and that tears are on-ly rain to make love grow. Well, my

tell by the way you hold me, dar-ling, _____ that it
love for you could nev-er grow no strong-er, _____ if I

won't be long be-fore it's cry-ing time. 2. Oh, they
live to be a hun-dred years _____ old. Oh, you

say that you found some-one you loved bet-ter, that's the

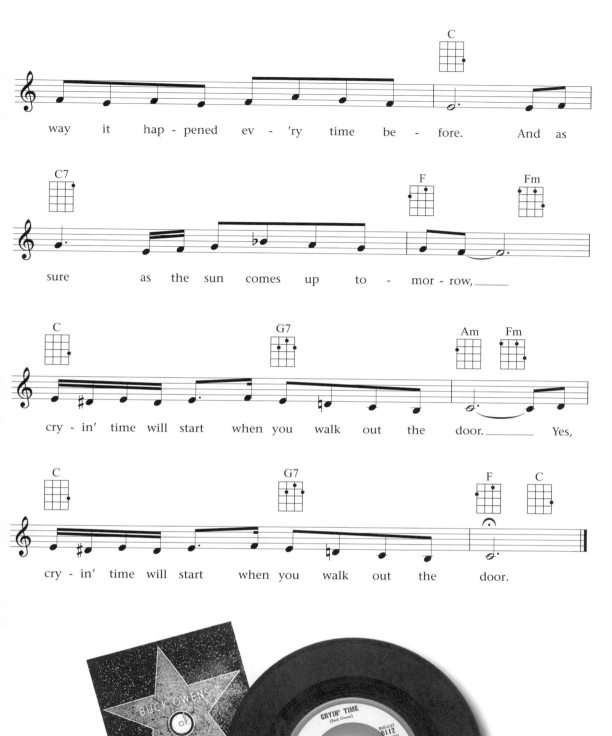

way it hap-pened ev-'ry time be - fore. And as

sure as the sun comes up to - mor - row,_____

cry - in' time will start when you walk out the door._____ Yes,

cry - in' time will start when you walk out the door.

Don't Fence Me In

Words and Music by
COLE PORTER

FIRST NOTE

Loping Along

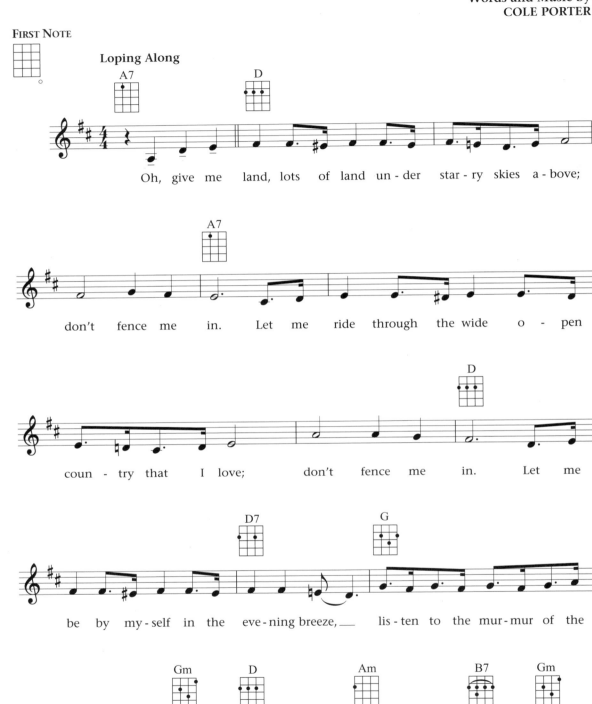

Oh, give me land, lots of land un-der star-ry skies a-bove; don't fence me in. Let me ride through the wide o-pen coun-try that I love; don't fence me in. Let me be by my-self in the eve-ning breeze, ___ lis-ten to the mur-mur of the

cot-ton-wood trees. ___ Send me off for-ev-er, but I ask you please, ___

Folsom Prison Blues

Words and Music by
JOHN R. CASH

FIRST NOTE

Moderately (not too slow)

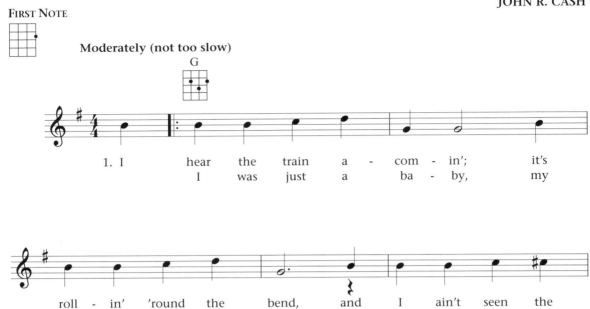

1. I hear the train a - com - in'; it's
   I was just a ba - by, my

roll - in' 'round the bend, and I ain't seen the
ma - ma told me, "Son, al - ways be a

sun - shine since I don't know when. I'm
good boy; don't ever play with guns." But I

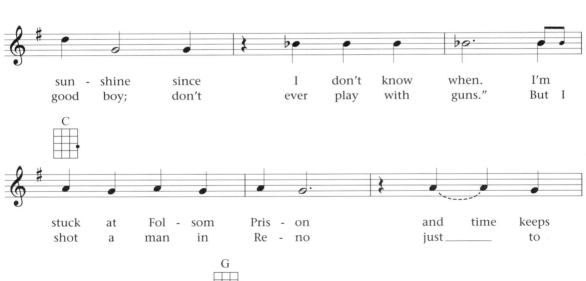

stuck at Fol - som Pris - on and time keeps
shot a man in Re - no just_____ to

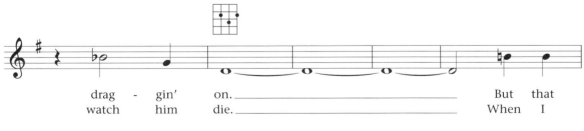

drag - gin' on. _____ But that
watch him die. _____ When I

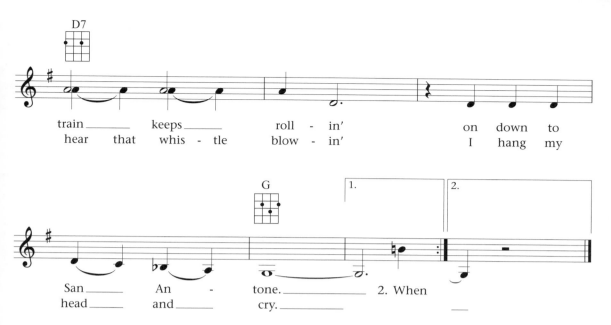

D7

train_____ keeps_____ roll - in'_____ on down to
hear that whis - tle blow - in' I hang my

G

1.
2.

San_____ An - tone._____ 2. When
head_____ and_____ cry._____

Additional Lyrics

3. I bet there's rich folks eatin' in a fancy dining car.
   They're prob'ly drinkin' coffee and smokin' big cigars,
   But I know I had it comin', I know I can't be free,
   But those people keep a-movin', and that's what tortures me.

4. Well, if they freed me from this prison, if that railroad train was mine,
   I bet I'd move on over a little farther down the line.
   Far from Folsom Prison, that's where I want to stay,
   And I'd let that lonesome whistle blow my blues away.

Galveston

Words and Music by
JIM WEBB

Gentle On My Mind

Words and Music by
JOHN HARTFORD

got-ten words and bonds___ and the ink stains that have dried up-on some

line. That___ keeps you in the back roads by the

riv-ers of my mem-'ry, that keeps you ev-er gen-tle on my

mind. 2. It's not

Additional Lyrics

2. It's not clinging to the rocks and ivy planted on their columns now that binds me
   Or something that somebody said because they thought we fit together walkin'.
   It's just knowing that the world will not be cursing or forgiving when I walk along
   Some railroad track and find
   That you're moving on the backroads by the rivers of my memory and for hours
   You're just gentle on my mind.

3. Though the wheat fields and the clothes lines and junkyards and the highways come between us
   And some other woman crying to her mother 'cause she turned and I was gone.
   I still run in silence, tears of joy might stain my face and summer sun might
   Burn me 'til I'm blind,
   But not to where I cannot see you walkin' on the backroads by the rivers flowing
   Gentle on my mind.

4. I dip my cup of soup back from the gurglin' cracklin' caldron in some train yard
   My beard a rough'ning coal pile and a dirty hat pulled low across my face.
   Through cupped hands 'round a tin can I pretend I hold you to my breast and find
   That you're waving from the backroads by the rivers of my memory ever smilin'
   Ever gentle on my mind.

(Ghost) Riders In The Sky

A Cowboy Legend

By STAN JONES

FIRST NOTE

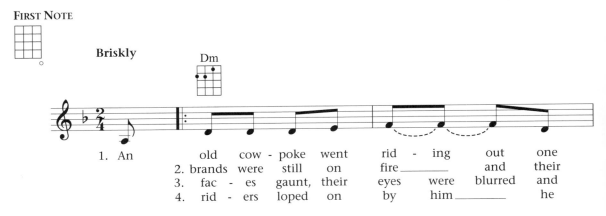

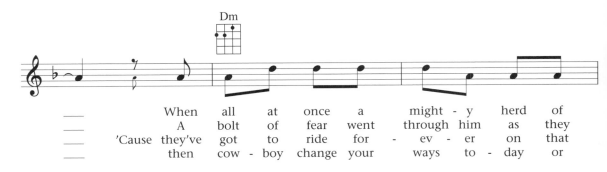

B♭

red - eyed cows he saw a - plough-in' thru the rag - ged skies___
thun - dered thru the sky, for he saw the rid - ers com - in' hard___
range up in the sky on hors - es snort - in' fire,___
with us you will ride a - try'n to catch the dev - il's herd___

Dm

_____
_____ and up a cloud - y draw.___
_____ and he heard their mourn - ful cry.___
_____ as they ride on, hear their cry."___
_____ a - cross these end - less skies."___

Dm7

⌐ 3 ¬

_____
_____ Yi - pi - yi - ay,_____
_____

Dm

⌐ 3 ¬

yi - pi - yi - o,_____ the

1.

B♭ **Gm7** **Dm**

1. ghost herd___ in___ the sky.___ 2. Their
2. ghost rid - ers in___ the sky.___ 3. Their
3. ghost rid - ers in___ the sky.___ 4. As the

2.

B♭ **Gm7** **Dm7**

4. ghost rid - ers in___ the sky._____

33

Green Green Grass Of Home

Words and Music by
CURLY PUTMAN

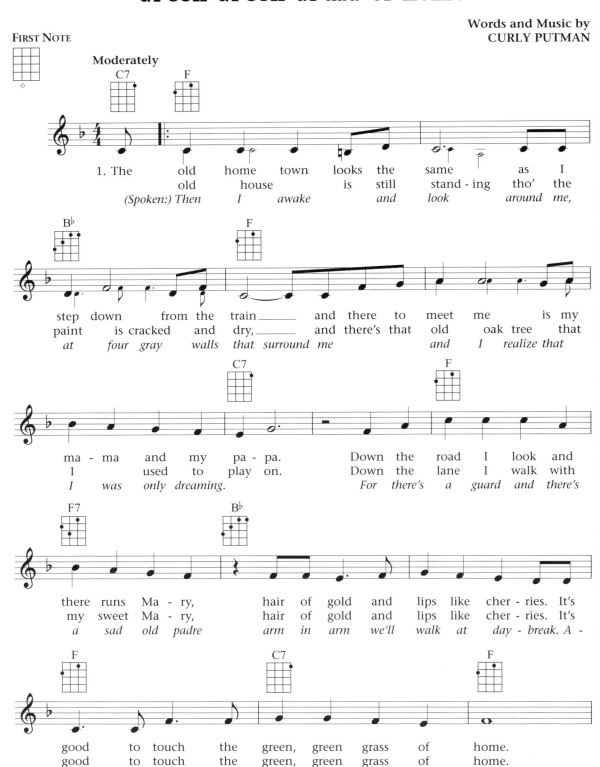

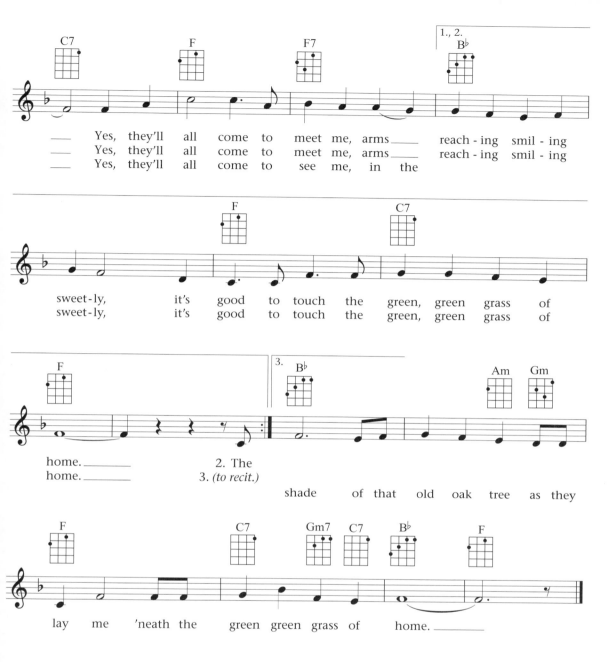

Yes, they'll all come to meet me, arms____ reach-ing smil-ing
Yes, they'll all come to meet me, arms____ reach-ing smil-ing
Yes, they'll all come to see me, in the

sweet-ly, it's good to touch the green, green grass of
sweet-ly, it's good to touch the green, green grass of

home._____ 2. The
home._____ 3. *(to recit.)*

shade of that old oak tree as they

lay me 'neath the green green grass of home. _____

A Typical Cabin,
near Knoxville, Tenn.

35

Happy Trails

FROM THE TELEVISION SERIES
"THE ROY ROGERS SHOW"

Words and Music by
DALE EVANS

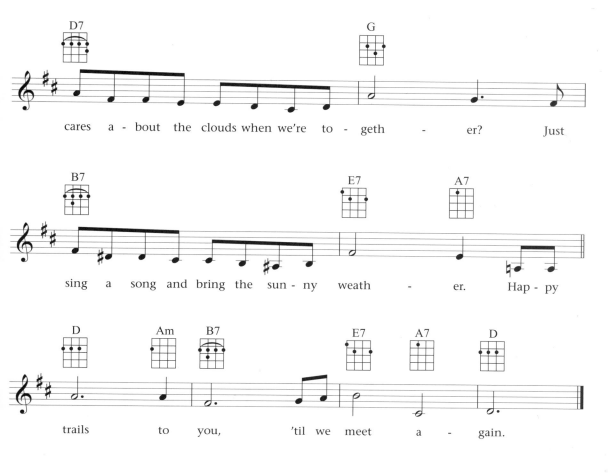

cares a - bout the clouds when we're to - geth — er? Just

sing a song and bring the sun - ny weath — er. Hap - py

trails to you, 'til we meet a - gain.

Heartaches By The Number

Words and Music by
HARLAN HOWARD

1. Heart - ache num - ber one was when you left me,
2. Heart - ache num - ber three was when you called me,

I nev - er knew that I could hurt this
and said that you were com - ing back to

way. And heart - ache num - ber two was when you -
stay. With hope - ful heart I wait - ed for your

came back a - gain, you came back and
knock on the door, I wait - ed but you

nev - er meant to stay. Now I've got
must have lost your way.

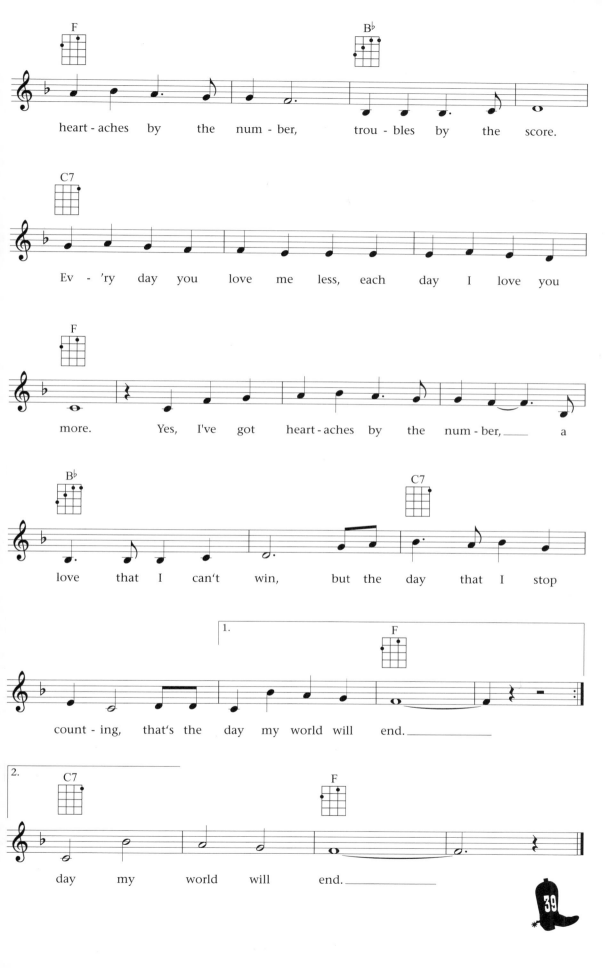

Hey, Good Lookin'

Words and Music by
HANK WILLIAMS

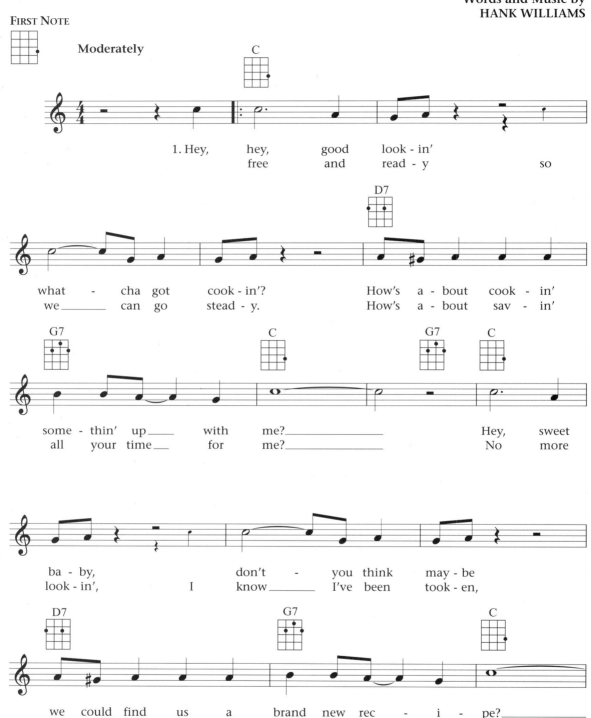

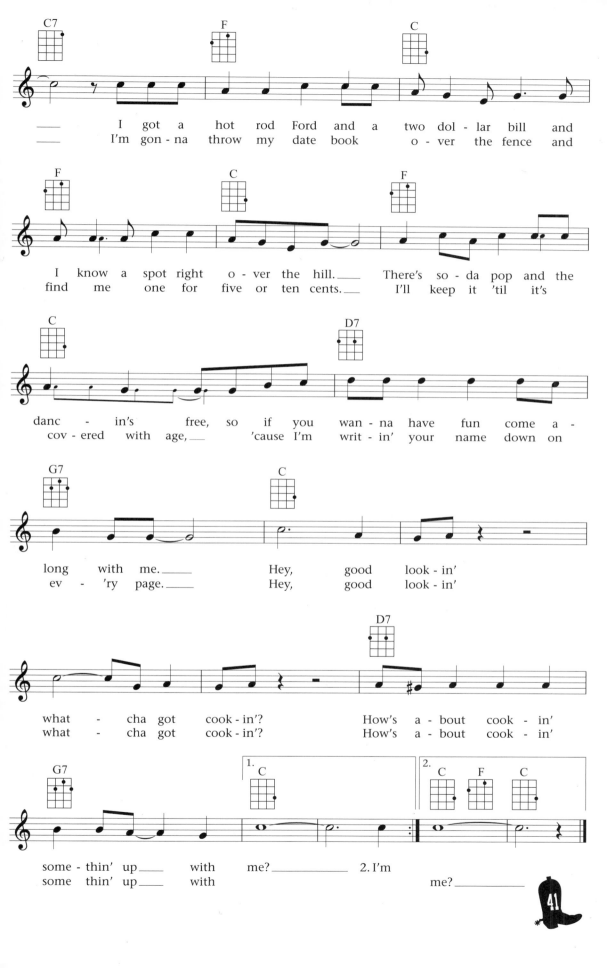

I Can't Stop Loving You

Words and Music by
DON GIBSON

FIRST NOTE

Slowly

Those hap-py hours _____ that we once knew, _____ _____ though long a-go, _____ still make me blue. _____ They say that time _____ heals _____ a bro-ken heart, _____ but time has stood still _____ since we've been a- part. _____ I can't stop lov-ing you, _____

so I've make up my mind ____ to live in mem-o-ry ____
there's no use to try. ____ Pre-tend there's some-one new; ____

of old lone-some times. ____ I can't stop
I can't live a lie. ____ I can't stop

want-ing you, ____ it's use-less to say, ____
want-ing you ____ the way that I do. ____

so I'll just live my life in dreams of yes-ter-
There's on-ly been one love for me, that one love is

1.
day. ____ 2. Those hap-py

2.
you. ____

I Fall To Pieces

Words and Music by
HANK COCHRAN and HARLAN HOWARD

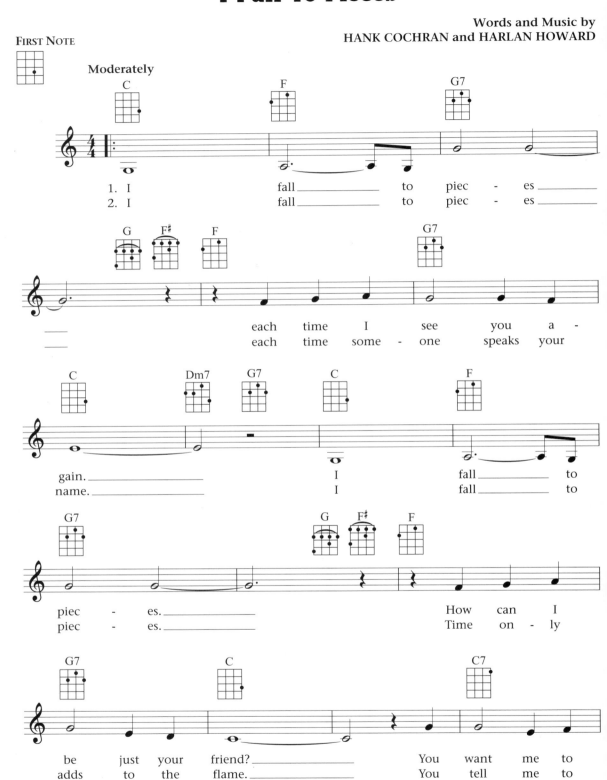

Moderately

1. I fall _____ to piec - es _____
2. I fall _____ to piec - es _____

each time I see you a -
each time some - one speaks your

gain. _____ I fall _____ to
name. _____ I fall _____ to

piec - es. _____ How can I
piec - es. _____ Time on - ly

be just your friend? _____ You want me to
adds to the flame. _____ You tell me to

F

act   like   we've   nev -   er kissed._____ You
find   some - one   else   to love._____ Some -

G7   **C**

want   me   to   for - get   pre - tend   we've   nev - er met._____
one   who'll love   me,   too,   the way   you   used   to do._____

C7   **F**   **G7**

___   And   I've   tried_____ and   I've   tried   but   I
___   But   each   time_____ I   go   out   with_____

C   **C7**   **F**   **G7**

have - n't yet._____ You walk   by   and   I   fall   to
some - one new._____ You walk   by   and   I   fall   to

1. **C**   **Dm7**   **G7**   **2.** **C**   **F**   **C**

piec - es._____   piec - es._____

45

I'm So Lonesome I Could Cry

Words and Music by
HANK WILLIAMS

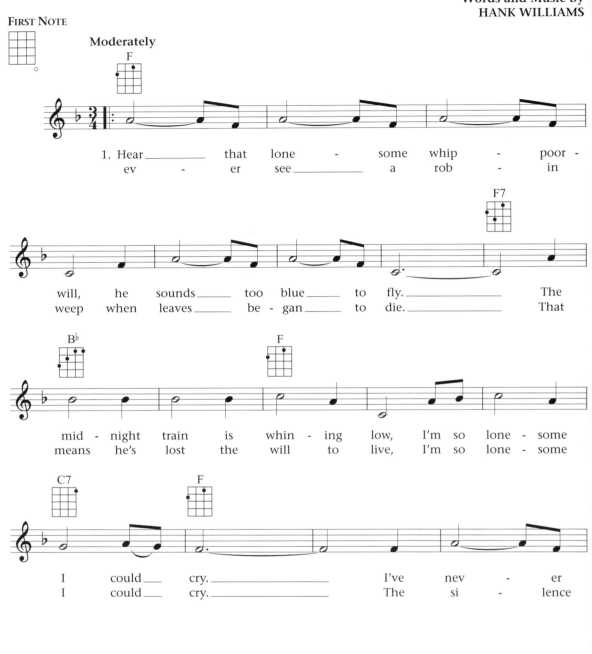

crawl - ing by. _____ The moon just
pur - ple sky. _____ And as I

went be - hind a cloud to ____ hide its
won - der where you are, I'm so lone - some

face and ____ cry. _____ 2. Did you
I could ____ cry. _____

Early 1950s photo of Hank Williams on guitar and Hank Williams Jr. on ukulele.

"A SONG AIN'T NOTHIN' IN THE WORLD BUT A STORY JUST WROTE WITH MUSIC TO IT."
— *Hank Williams*

47

King Of The Road

Words and Music by
ROGER MILLER

FIRST NOTE

Moderately Slow

1., 3. Trail - er_____ for sale or rent;_____
2. Third box - car mid - night train;_____

rooms_____ to let,_____ fif - ty cents;_____
des - ti - na - tion Ban - gor, Maine._____

no phone,_____ no pool, no pets;_____ I ain't got no
Old worn - out suit and shoes;_____ I don't pay no

ci - ga - rettes._____ Ah, but two hours_____ of
un - ion dues._____ I smoke old sto - gies

push - ing broom_____ buys an eight_____ by twelve_____
I have found,_____ short_____ but not too

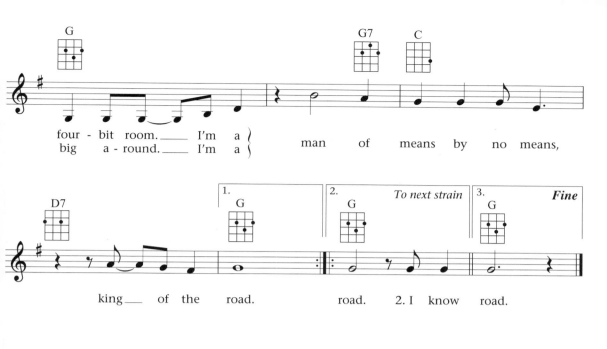

four - bit room.___ I'm a } big a - round.___ I'm a }

man of means by no means,

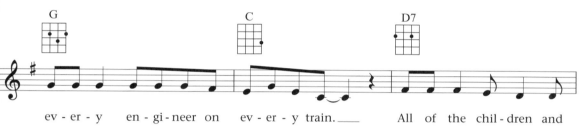

king___ of the road.

road. 2. I know road.

ev - er - y en - gi - neer on ev - er - y train.___ All of the chil - dren and

all of their names, ___ and ev - er - y hand - out in ev - er - y town, ___ and

D.S. al Fine

ev - 'ry lock that ain't locked when no one's a - round. 3. I sing

★ **"I WRITE LIKE I TALK."** ★
— *Roger Miller*

On The Road Again

Words and Music by
WILLIE NELSON

road a - gain,＿＿＿＿ like a band of gyp - sies

we go down the high - way.＿＿＿＿ We're the

best of friends,＿＿ in - sist - ing that the world keep turn - ing

our way,＿＿＿＿ and our way,＿＿＿＿ is on the

road a - gain.＿＿＿＿＿＿ Just can't wait to get on the

road a - gain.＿＿＿＿＿＿＿ The life I

51

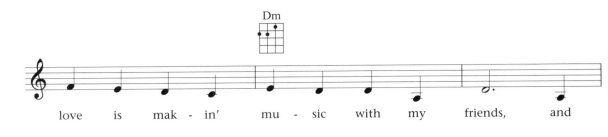

love   is   mak - in'   mu - sic   with   my   friends,   and

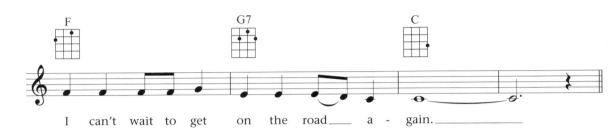

I   can't   wait   to   get   on   the   road___ a - gain.___

Ragtime Cowboy Joe

Words by
GRANT CLARKE

Music by LEWIS F. MUIR
and MAURICE ABRAHAMS

A7

hear that fel - low's gun, be - cause the West - ern folks all know; he's a

Em

high - fa - lut - ing, scoot - ing, shoot - ing son - of - a - gun from Ar - i - zo - na,

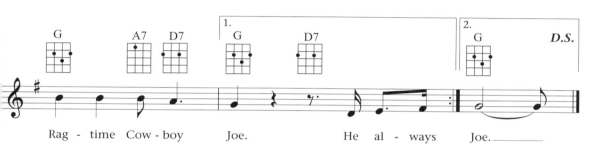

G   A7   D7   1. G   D7   2. G   D.S.

Rag - time Cow - boy   Joe.   He al - ways   Joe._____

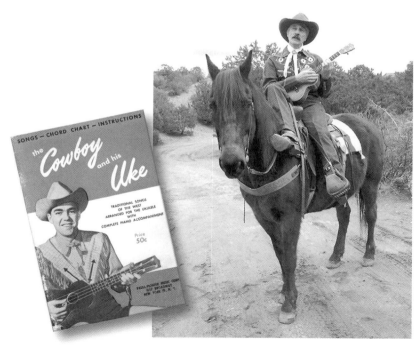

1950s songbook The Cowboy And His Uke. *Western singer and uke player, Sid Hausman, strums on horseback (2005).*

Ring Of Fire

Words and Music by
MERLE KILGORE and JUNE CARTER

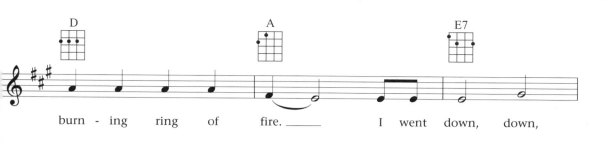

burn - ing   ring   of   fire. _____   I   went   down,   down,

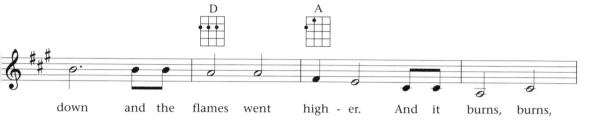

down   and   the   flames   went   high - er.   And   it   burns,   burns,

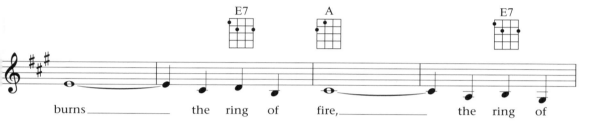

burns _____   the   ring   of   fire, _____   the   ring   of

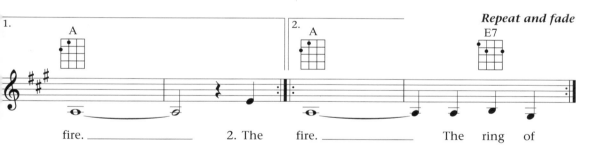

fire. _____   2. The   fire. _____   The   ring   of

Ryman Auditorium in Nashville, home of the
Grand Ole Opry *from 1943-1974.*

Rocky Top

Words and Music by
BOUDLEAUX BRYANT and FELICE BRYANT

FIRST NOTE

Lively

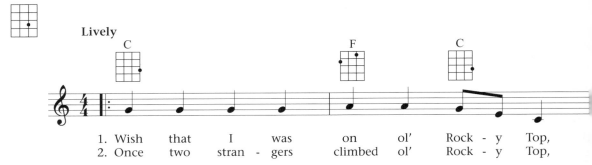

1. Wish that I was on ol' Rock - y Top,
2. Once two stran - gers climbed ol' Rock - y Top,

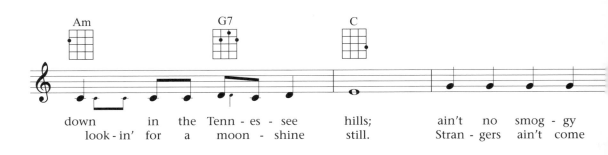

down in the Tenn - es - see hills; ain't no smog - gy
look - in' for a moon - shine still. Stran - gers ain't come

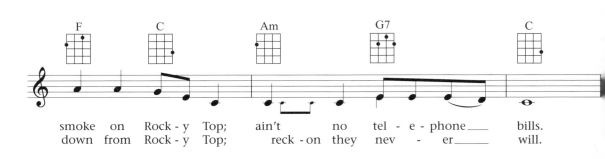

smoke on Rock - y Top; ain't no tel - e - phone____ bills.
down from Rock - y Top; reck - on they nev - er____ will.

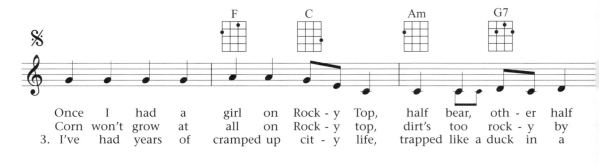

Once I had a girl on Rock - y Top, half bear, oth - er half
Corn won't grow at all on Rock - y top, dirt's too rock - y by
3. I've had years of cramped up cit - y life, trapped like a duck in a

Singing The Blues

Words and Music by
MELVIN ENDSLEY

FIRST NOTE

Moderate swing

Well, I nev-er felt more like sing-ing the blues, ___ 'cause

I nev-er thought ___ that I'd ev-er lose ___ your love, dear.

Why'd you do me this way? _____ Well, I nev-er felt more like

cry-ing all night, ___ 'cause ev-'ry-thing's wrong, ___ and noth-ing ain't right ___ with-

out you. You got me sing-ing the blues. _____ The

moon and stars no long-er shine; the dream is gone I thought was mine. There's

noth-ing left for me to do but cry

o-ver you. Well, I nev-er felt more like run-ning a-way, but

why should I go, 'cause I could-n't stay with-out you?

You got me sing-ing the blues.

Stand By Your Man

Words and Music by
TAMMY WYNETTE and BILLY SHERRILL

1. Some-times it's hard to be a wom-an,
2. But if you love him, you'll for-give him,

___ giv-ing all your love to just one man.
___ e-ven though he's hard to un-der-stand. ___

You'll have bad times, and he'll have
And if you love him,

good times, do-in' things that you don't un-der-

1. stand. ___

2. oh, ___ be proud of him,

*optional – x means don't play that string

San Antonio Rose

Words and Music by
BOB WILLS

Deep with - in my heart lies a mel - o -
dy, a song of old San An - tone,_____ where in
dreams I live with a mem - o - ry, be -
neath the stars all a - lone._____ It was
there I found be - side the Al - a - mo en -

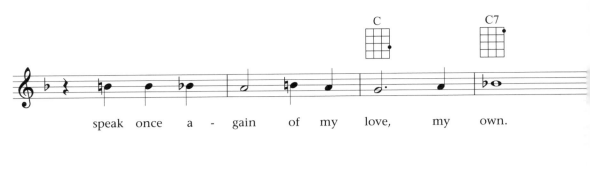

speak once a - gain of my love, my own.

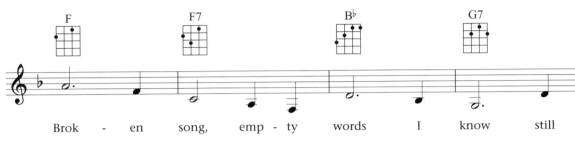

Brok - en song, emp - ty words I know still

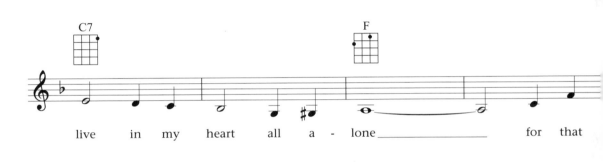

live in my heart all a - lone _____ for that

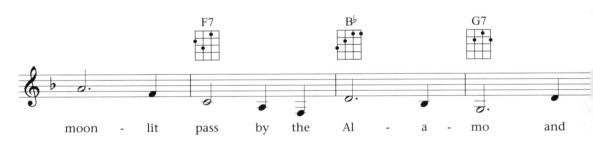

moon - lit pass by the Al - a - mo and

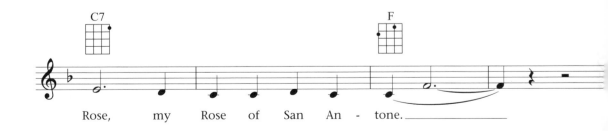

Rose, my Rose of San An - tone. _____

Take Me Home, Country Roads

Words and Music by BILL DANOFF,
TAFFY NIVERT and JOHN DENVER

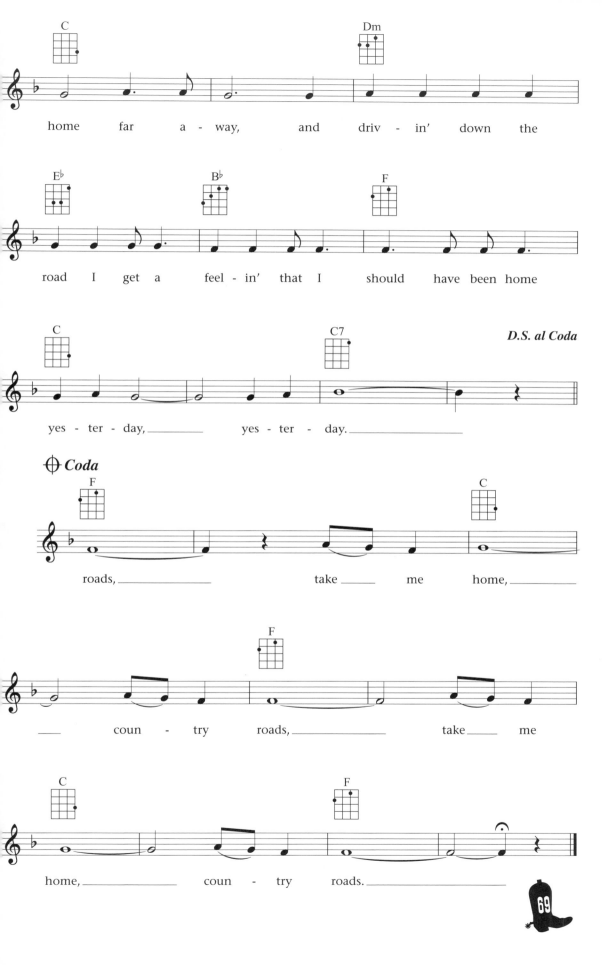

Tennessee Waltz

Words and Music by
REDD STEWART and PEE WEE KING

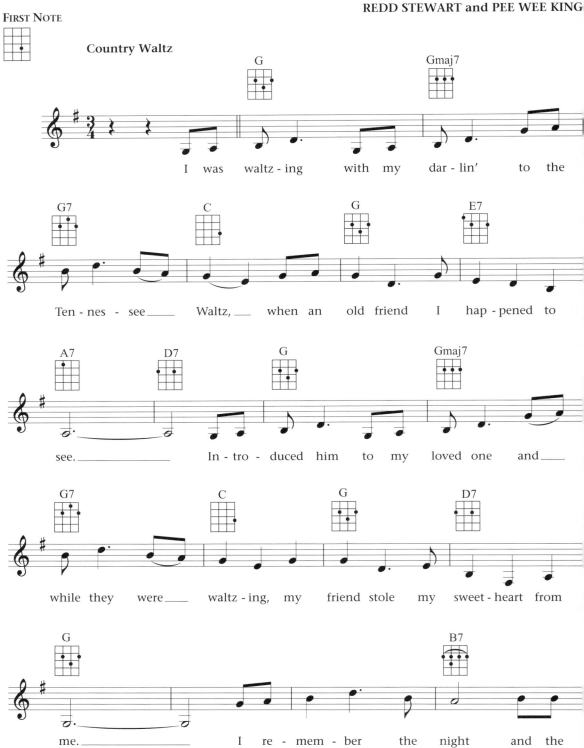

Country Waltz

I was waltz - ing with my dar - lin' to the Ten - nes - see___ Waltz,___ when an old friend I hap - pened to see.___ In - tro - duced him to my loved one and___ while they were___ waltz - ing, my friend stole my sweet - heart from me.___ I re - mem - ber the night and the

| C | G | E7 |

Ten - nes - see Waltz. Now I know just how much I have

| A7 | D7 | G |

lost._____ Yes I lost my lit - tle

| G7 | C |

dar - lin' the____ night they were____ play - ing the

| G | D7 | G |

beau - ti - ful Ten - nes - see Waltz._____

Tennessee Waltz
By REDD STEWART and PEE WEE KING
RECORDED BY PATTI PAGE FOR MERCURY RECORDS

PUBLISHED BY
ACUFF-ROSE PUBLICATIONS, INC.
Sole Selling Agent
ACUFF-ROSE SALES, INC.
2510 FRANKLIN ROAD
NASHVILLE 4, TENNESSEE

Featured by
PATTI PAGE

71

Tumbling Tumbleweeds

Words and Music by
BOB NOLAN

I'm___ a roam-ing cow-boy, rid - ing all day long,

tum - ble-weeds a - round me sing___ their lone - ly song.

Nights un-der-neath a prai-rie moon, I ride a-lone and sing a tune.

See___ them tum - bling down, pledg - ing their love to the ground,

lone - ly but free I'll be found, drift - ing a-long with the tum - bling

tum - ble weeds. __ Cares __ of the past are be - hind, no - where to go, but I'll

find just __ where the trail __ will wind, drift - ing a-long with the tumb - ling

tum - ble weeds. ___ I ___ know ___ when night has gone that a

new ___ world's born at dawn. I'll ___ keep roll - ing a -

long, deep ___ in my heart is a song; here ___ on the range I be -

long, drift - ing a - long with the tum - bling tum-ble weeds. __

73

Walkin' After Midnight

Words by
DON HECHT

Music by
ALAN W. BLOCK

74

You Are My Sunshine

Words and Music by
JIMMIE DAVIS

1. The oth - er night dear _____ as I lay
2. love you _____ and make you
3. once dear _____ you real - ly

sleep - ing, _____ I dreamed I held you
hap - py. _____ If you will on - ly
loved me, _____ and no one else could

in my arms. _____ When I a -
say the same, _____ but if you
come be - tween, _____ but now you've

woke dear _____ I was mis - tak - en _____
leave me _____ to love an - oth - er _____
left me _____ and love an - oth - er _____

_____ and I hung my head and
_____ you'll re - gret it all some
_____ you have shat - tered all my

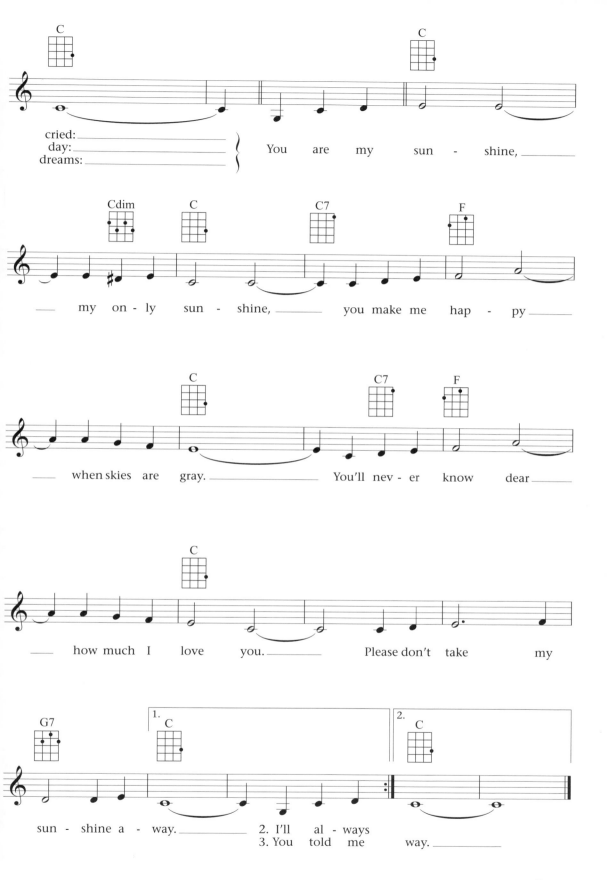

cried: _____
day: _____
dreams: _____

You are my sun - shine, _____ my on - ly sun - shine, _____ you make me hap - py _____ when skies are gray. _____ You'll nev - er know dear _____ how much I love you. _____ Please don't take my

1. sun - shine a - way. _____
2. I'll al - ways
3. You told me way. _____

Your Cheatin' Heart

Words and Music by
HANK WILLIAMS

G · · · G7 · · · C · · ·

you._____ When tears come down_____
you._____ When tears come down_____

G · · ·

____ like fall - in' rain,_____ you'll toss a -
____ like fall - in' rain,_____ you'll toss a -

A7 · · · D7 · · ·

round _____ and call my name._____
round _____ and call my name._____

G · · · G7 · · ·

____ You'll walk the____ floor_____ the way I
____ You'll walk the____ floor_____ the way I

C · · · D7 · · ·

do, _____ your cheat - in'____ heart_____ will tell on
do, _____ your cheat - in'____ heart_____ will tell on

1. · · · G · · · D7 · · · | 2. · · · G · · ·

you._____ 2. Your cheat - in'____ | you._____

Old In New Mexico

Words by
JIM BELOFF

Music by
LYLE RITZ

FIRST NOTE

Moderately

1. When we've been ev - 'ry place to be, __ and we've seen ev - 'ry - thing to see, __
2. It's a place where it rare - ly rains, __ so it's good for our aches and pains. __

___ then we would like to grow ___ old in New Mex - i - co. ___
___ Yes, we would like to grow ___ old in New Mex - i - co. ___ With my señ - o - ra

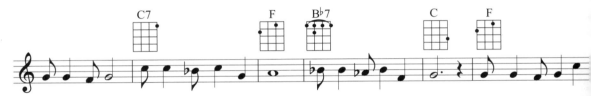

in San - ta Fe, there in that west - ern town, home of a - do - be brown, we'll watch the sun go

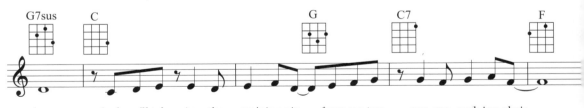

down. And we'll take in the ev - 'ning air, __ from our two - per - son rock - ing chair. __

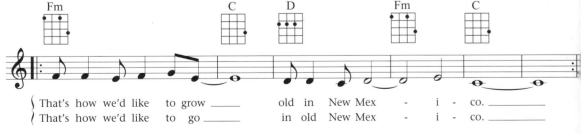

That's how we'd like to grow ___ old in New Mex - i - co. ___
That's how we'd like to go ___ in old New Mex - i - co. ___